Your Pot of Gold
is a
Handshake Away!

A Step-by-Step Plan for Quickly Growing Your Business Through Referrals

By

Linda Ballesteros

ISBN: 978-1-105-68175-2

ACKNOWLEDGEMENTS

My deepest gratitude goes to my husband and soul mate, Mario, for his faith in me and constant encouragement. He believed in me before I believed in myself.

I want to thank those members of the networking community who unknowingly contributed to my lessons in the right and wrong ways of building relationships through networking.

Table of Contents

Introduction vii

Community/Relationships 1

Confidence 23

Consistency 43

Positive Outlook 65

Ethics and Values 75

Vision 95

Introduction

An Amazingly Powerful yet Simple Strategy
for Building a Business Based on Referrals

If you are a business owner, entrepreneur, or anyone responsible for driving new clients to your business, don't just read this book—make it an integral part of your business life, devour the concepts, and memorize the portions that resonate with you.

This book reveals concepts that can literally change your life. You will learn powerful strategies for "pulling" new clients toward you, rather than "pushing" them with the same old sales tactics.

Learn this strategy—it can easily be learned—and you can expect certain immediate benefits:

- You will never have to feel that you are chasing the next lead.
- Clients will become important relationships.
- The demand for your product or service will skyrocket.
- As a result, you will earn more money—perhaps multiples of what you are earning now.

If that weren't enough, you will also:

- Stop wasting time working with customers who don't know your value to them, and
- Experience the peace of knowing you will have a constant stream of referral business.

After reading this book, you will be able to put some important tools and techniques to work. The book is designed for you to take action on a single principle at a time in order to instill a lifestyle change that produces enjoyment and profit.

By keeping this book as a personal resource, you won't have to worry about forgetting any of the details. Everything you need to understand about this lifestyle is contained in the following pages.

How Was This Idea Developed?

As the leader of several networking organizations, I have had the opportunity to coach many of my members about the value of growing their business through referral marketing.

The question I ask is:

Would you like for me to buy your product or would you like for me to introduce you to hundreds of potential customers?

That is exactly what a referral partner can do for you and your business.

The perfect referral partner carries magic dust that can explode your business in a way years of time and thousands of dollars could never produce.

The American Marketing Association states:

"Over 90% of C-level executive (Chief Financial Officer, Chief Operating Officer, Chief fill in the blank Officer) never or almost never respond to e-mail blasts and cold-calls. But over 80% of them do engage when referred by a connection – whether through a friend, colleague, customer or industry peer."

Now do you see the power of referral marketing and the value of finding the perfect partner?

What Most Networking Teachers Won't Teach You

This book is about developing an attitude toward new business development that is worlds apart from what is promoted in many networking organizations. Our goal is to teach the *BIG* things that attract people to work with you.

Big things like:

- How to emotionally connect with the ideal client.
- What methods you can use to show sincere appreciation for referrals in a way that motivates them to send you more.
- Why you desire referrals from others and how that desire can fuel your activities to grow your business.

This way of referral business is different from the reciprocal obligation to give and receive leads. It bypasses the intellectual logic of earning an exchange of referrals and goes to the heart of why people *WANT* to tell others about what you offer.

How to Use This Book

If you are like most people, you will read (or at least scan) most of this book immediately. If that is all you do, you have just wasted your money in buying the book. You should have used the money to take a potential client to lunch.

Transformation is the goal of this book. Transformation takes time and intention. That is why we designed the book to include:

- A quote from someone famous that you may respect,
- An expansion of the quote's concept as it relates to business by referral, and
- Exercises that can cause specific actions that will embed the concept on a deeper level into your lifestyle.
- Carry a journal with you to gather valuable information about your progress.

If you follow these steps, there is no doubt in my mind that your goal of transformation will be achieved.

You will earn more money and attain sure confidence that your business will continue to expand.

Community/Relationships

Keep Them Happy

Client relationships are perhaps the most important aspect in deciding the fate of your business. In fact, your current clients are your best referral partners. Many don't really realize the importance of client relationships in a business.

I recently read a book that described how most of us want and need the feeling of being a part of a community. This is in spite of the fact that many live in the suburbs, behind security gates and in large, secluded homes. Take a look at the explosion of Facebook and other online social media sites and you will know what I mean.

Taking care of your client is the foundation of growing your business because your clients are your community. That is why maintaining or improving client relationships will benefit you tenfold.

Let them know that you appreciate them and their business with more than the obligatory Christmas card. Congratulate them when you notice a Facebook post about a birthday celebration, wedding, anniversary, etc.

Offer them gifts and discounts from time to time to make sure that they feel "your business values them" as opposed to "you value their business." Everyone loves these little things. It is the best way you can continue to build client relationships.

"Reach out and touch someone."

—AT&T

Every once in a while you will find profound wisdom in advertising. This phrase was indelibly etched into the American psyche and countless phone calls to family or friends were made as people thought of how important it was to touch other people's lives.

I haven't heard that slogan in some time. Perhaps it became ineffective for selling long-distance services after so many years. However, we still need to reach out and touch others, with warm thoughts, a simple hello, and an encouraging word. I am learning, as I mature, that relationships are all that really matter.

I struggle with recognizing that my priorities are misaligned if I spend all my time earning a living and rarely find time to develop deep and meaningful relationships with others. The magic of the referral process is that we can develop those relationships with clients and friends at the same time that we are growing our business.

Allow time in your days that are specifically scheduled to reach others. First, let them know that you care about them by asking about their lives, their businesses, and families. Second, remind them of the important role that they play in your business and your success. Before you hang up the phone, as an "Oh by the way," tell them that you are never too busy for their referrals. Record those that you "touched" in your journal with a few words about each conversation. Follow up with a personal note.

"The greatest good you can do for another is not just to share your riches, but to reveal to him his own."

—Benjamin Disraeli

Part of being in business is the daily "hit" from someone wanting your money. People think that owning a business or being in sales naturally takes you into the realms of the rich. Every schoolchild and every nonprofit agency comes with hand outstretched, asking for your hard-earned money.

The "Law of Reciprocity" dictates that there is a cyclical motion to everything. In order to receive, you must first give. Naturally, you must give to others to have a referral based business—but what gift is most valuable?

Part of the referral mindset is giving your fellow business partners referrals. That is easy. But there is so much more you can bring to this person with whom you have developed a referral partnership. You may offer him a mirror in which to see his gifts and blessings.

No longer are your business relationships distant and impersonal. By reflecting the "riches" that they possess, you can contribute untold pleasures to other people's lives. Change the lives of others by helping them recognize their own "riches." What a prosperous life!

Resolve to make a difference in the lives of others. Keep track of the sincere compliments offered to clients, employees, and friends. Try to offer at least three validating compliments each day by extending a professional compliment to someone, either in person, sending an e-mail, or simply posting a comment on social media.

"People are best convinced by ideas that they come to by themselves."

—Ben Franklin

In our age of "No-Call" lists, it is apparent that people do not want to listen to your reasons why they should buy your latest and greatest product or service. The construction of barriers between consumer and purveyor of goods or services is building at a rapid pace.

This phenomenon is a natural extension of the screening device, formerly known as an answering machine. When people purchased answering machines in the 60s, it was because they were afraid someone would call and they would not know about it. Voice mail was originally for the purpose of capturing all calls.

As voice mail has become an integral part of most households and businesses, it is serving a completely different function. Now the role of voice mail systems is primarily to screen calls. It enables people to be more selective about who gets their precious time and attention.

Every business benefits from referrals, but not everyone understands why they work so effectively. Take time to educate your clients about why referrals are valuable to them. When they send you people who need your product or service, you can actually spend more time working for them and their needs. Without referrals from good people, you have to constantly spend time in finding new clients. Make sure your best clients know it is in their best interest to duplicate themselves.

Think about the people you know who would be willing to refer you. Why would they make the effort to "spread good rumors" about you? List the benefits to those people who might refer you, then teach those reasons to those willing referral sources. Try this with at least two people in your referral pool and describe your experiences in your journal.

"Remember, if you ever need a helping hand, you'll find one at the end of your arm...
As you grow older
you will discover that you
have two hands...
one for helping yourself,
the other for helping others."

—Audrey Hepburn

If you have experienced any measure of success, you know that it comes from helping yourself first. You must work with zeal and much effort. You must do the things that need to be done by you.

One of the indescribable joys of developing a referral community is the opportunity to watch others develop and grow as well. As you get to know more about the individuals in your client base, you can reach back and help someone who understands the "Law of Reciprocity." You have the opportunity to watch that seed of helping blossom into great prosperity for them. As the giving comes full circle, you are again blessed by their success. Their success becomes your celebration and the magic unfolds.

Gary Keller, Chairman of the Board of Keller Williams Realty, teaches that no one has become a success by himself. Sure, you may have worked very hard and should take the time to celebrate that success. Then it is time to reach back, help another, and then feel the warmth of the hand in front of you, helping you to even greater heights.

Look around and discover those who could benefit from the referral process. Contact at least one business person before the end of the week and introduce him to this way of creating a referral-based business. Ask him specific questions about his needs and find ways to help him reach his goals. Then encourage him to pass the blessings on to the next person and anticipate the return of blessings to you. Record the name(s) of people you contacted in your journal, and by each name, write the result of the exchange.

**"*Live by the 'Three Foot Rule'
Surround yourself with people
who will enhance you spiritually,
emotionally, intellectually
and professionally.*"**

**—*Dave Jenks, Keller Williams
University***

We become who we associate with. If you want to be someone who is growing and learning from year to year, put yourself in a learning-based environment. If you want to become more spiritual, surround yourself with spiritually-enlightened people. It sounds so very simple. Monitor who gets within three feet of your personal space because those people have great influence on your life.

It may be simple, but it is not always easy. As training coach, Brian Buffini, says, "Keep putting the good stuff in." Through the process of growing intellectually and professionally, by attending seminars, listening to tapes, and reading books, you will find others seeking you out as someone they would like to associate with.

This makes you someone they want to refer business to, simply because you have made yourself a better person.

Try this exercise. In your journal, list the people you associate with each day at work, at home, and in your leisure time. Then beside each name, indicate whether they have a positive attitude. Do you select people to be around you who stimulate you to achieve more?

Now, don't go and tell people that they must get out of your life because they have a negative attitude. Instead, work on yourself. Be the one with the positive attitude. Seek your spiritual center and become composed with God's love for you and those around you.

"It is individuals in community that create the greatest value – strong individuals in strong relationships."

—Rosabeth Moss Kanter, author of Evolve: Succeeding in the Digital Culture of Tomorrow

"Building strong relationships with my referral partners have been key to growing my business. By taking the time to really understand their 'why' and their goals, I find it much easier to find referrals to give. In turn, this builds incredible trust between us, and my business has flourished."

—Diana Boulanger
Arbonne International
Spring, Tx

Several decades ago, we moved from the small community existence into the industrial age. In the new culture, value was placed on being a part of the larger picture. Decisions were made from the "top," and the masses were expected to respond by doing their own part, with gratitude for a regular paycheck and looking forward to a retirement in the future.

As that way of life unravels into diminished investment portfolios and forced entry into the workplace, many people feel betrayed by the system that valued following the rules. Today's rapid rate of change has thrown us into a brand-new world, a world with very different opportunities and very different responsibilities.

Today, we are responsible for making judgments about what is right and wrong for us, on an individual basis. There are no rules we can follow to assure us of continued employment, much less any hope for guaranteed retirement income.

Visualize a perfect world full of strong relationships. Use your journal to describe this world full of people who engaged in your life in a meaningful way. Be very descriptive as you outline this time and place. Focus on how it feels to be part of a community with others. Have confidence that this outcome is possible. In fact, you know it is coming soon, because you hold the vision and have faith in its reality.

---

*"We live in a world in which we need to share responsibility. It's easy to say 'It's not my community…not my problem.' Then there are those who see the need and respond.
I consider those people my heroes."*

**—Fred Rogers, host of
Mister Rogers' Neighborhood**

The greater vision for doing business by referral is one of literally changing the way that business is conducted. At times, it feels as distant as the concept of "world peace." But, the concept is indeed working in numerous business environments around the United States. The concept is growing like wildfire and I believe that it is possible that we can be instruments of change in a world that craves connections with other people.

The fact that your business profitability will increase is an incredible by-product of living a more useful and significant life. Think about how you can make the lives of your customers a little better.

How could you treat your best customers if you did not have those picky, complaining, and impossible people demanding ever more from you? If you delete the unreasonable clients from your business, you could treat the best customers with a sense of caring that you cannot currently afford to spend. So start today. Sort your database. List the clients who are loyal to you. The ones who appreciate you when you do more deserve your very best effort. Delete customers who cannot be pleased. Treat your best customers as if they were made of gold, then teach them how to give you referrals. They will respond by recommending you to people they know, therefore duplicating themselves. Guess what kind of people nice people know?

This is it! Now is the time to look through your entire database and delete any customer you would not like to have duplicated! Be brave; your good customers and clients deserve to be selected and served at the highest level. Record your experience in your journal.

"I thought people would simply use the service to buy and sell things, but what they really enjoyed was meeting other people."

—Pierre Omidya, founder of eBay

Relationships...what is more important than our connection to other people? Life is so busy that getting the immediate family to set aside time to connect can seem to be an insurmountable challenge. And without those deep relationships, some people are starving for more human connection.

With today's technology, corporations are cutting operating costs by having employees work from home. In addition, one of the fastest-growing aspects of our economy is entrepreneurship. Many have chosen self-employment as a way to provide income opportunities, even if it means becoming disconnected and isolated in the process. Other people have "retired," only to find that they miss the connection with others that employment provided.

These and other factors have created a culture of people who have an intense craving to be part of a community. Countless hours are spent making a living, so being part of a business community that generates reciprocal leads nourishes us in more ways than just income. These relationships connect us with something much greater. While we are "making a living," we are also "making a life" that is rewarding.

Think about the things you currently do to develop deep and meaningful relationships. Have you let that aspect of your life take a backseat to all the other demands in your life? Examine the things that you enjoy on a personal basis that connect you with others. Select one or two things that will add a sense of connection to your life. Start this week to implement one of those activities. Begin now and know that this deliberate activity will bring pleasure to your life, while enriching the lives of those you encounter. Observe how your life changes when you deliberately connect with others. At the end of the week, record your experiences in your journal.

"That's how it is with people sometimes. When you least expect it, a common thread – golden at that – begins to weave together the fabric of friendship."
—Mary Kay Shanley

"I received an e-mail to meet with some business coaches at our Mary Kay seminar in Dallas this past summer. I met the business-coaching couple in August. I hired them as my coach, and one of my friends hired them as well.

The Houston area Mary Kay organization was looking for a speaker for our January Jumpstart Event – and we hired them. Over 200 people heard them—and they generated LOTS of present business AND future business!

"All because of networking! I love it. AND—I love connecting people and businesses!"

—Mary Taylor
Mary Kay Cosmetics
Katy, Tx

Looking for people who belong in your referral network can be an unpredictable process. At some point, the relationships with your referral sources will, more than likely, become friendships. That is part of the "magic" in this way of doing business. You are able to receive validation from those friendships and validate their gifts as well.

You have probably seen people who change as the years pass. At an early age, before wisdom and maturity become a part of their business, they pursue money, fame, and self-validation. If they are lucky, they mature and find that the richness of life comes from more permanent things—like the value of someone who really knows you, likes you, and trusts you.

Knowing that others place a value on what you bring to their lives is gratifying on an emotional level—and profitable in a financial way. Seek out those people to do business with.

One goal of the referral process is to create a community of "friends" who believe in the value you offer and want to be a part of your success. What an incredibly beautiful way to live your life!

Look for the common thread in the people you meet. Not all you encounter will be chosen to be a part of your referral community. Be selective about who you let come into your life and have faith. The golden threads are out there, just waiting to make your life richer.

What people are you doing business with who have become friends? In your journal, create a page that lists those friendships. Answer these three questions: What do these people have in common? What can you do to let them know how golden the thread is between you? What can you do to duplicate this kind of person in your life? Now go out to find more people with the same qualities to add to your networking circle.

Two are better than one; because they have a good reward for their labour.

For if they fall, the one will lift up his fellow: but woe to him that is alone when he falleth; for he hath not another to help him up.

—King James Version Bible.

This passage from the Old Testament is just as true today as it was in the ancient times when it was written. Independence is admired in our culture. Some claim to be "self-made." I truly pity the perceived success of people who feel that they have reached a prominent position of notoriety without the assistance of others.

Most of us would like to think that we can accomplish great things through our own doing. But, the fact is, I don't know of anyone I admire who doesn't admit to being helped by many people around them. They are not being overly modest. Instead, a part of reaching true success is recognizing the talent of those who have supported and encouraged the efforts of others along the way.

What the "lone ranger" types in the world do not understand is that not only can you accomplish more when you are able to engage others in your efforts, but that the true beauty is in the relationships developed in the tasks. What good is it to reach a goal and not have your peers rejoicing in your achievement?

Engage as many people as you can in your success. If you are truly following the "Law of Reciprocity," they will be happy to be a part of your continued success.

Who has been "the wind beneath your wings"? Take time this week to contact the people who have supported your goals and helped you to achieve. Tell them how important they are to your success. Follow up your call (or better yet, your face-to-face meeting) with a personal note of appreciation. You may make a significant impact on the life of someone who has been beneficial to you.

Confidence

Strengthen Your Courage Muscle

Reflecting on a conversation this morning reminded me that lack of confidence is an issue for many. It is true for solopreneurs and solo practitioners everywhere, and it certainly isn't exclusive to those who engage business and personal coaches. The ironic part is that many of them believe they are the only ones struggling with the fears associated with a lack of confidence. Oftentimes, it isn't until they enter into a coaching relationship that people discover confidence is lacking. It is lacking in large numbers across ranks of entrepreneurs and high-achieving executives everywhere.

Those who struggle with confidence often build barriers that keep them from taking the emotional risks associated with business growth. Business owners will do only what is necessary to reach the border of their tolerance levels, known as the comfort zone. They will manufacture many excuses to stay within those *safe* confines—and yet, so much more is possible.

Comfort zones come in all shapes and sizes. For some, living within their comfort zones still allow for measured success and a steady income—even strong profits in many cases. In sports, it's called "playing to NOT LOSE, instead of playing to WIN." For others, the dream remains a dream and, tragically, may never see the light of day. Lack of confidence lurks inside the comfort zone, keeping you from your greatest potential.

It is time now to strengthen your courage muscle and venture outside your comfort zone.

Confidence, relationships, and profits await!

"When it rains, I let it."
—A 113-year-old man who was asked the secret of his longevity

The answer to a question asked at a seminar I attended helped me to eliminate worry. Take the next few minutes, notice the date, and try to recall what you were worrying about this time last year. Chances are you don't even have a clue. In fact, whatever concern you were worrying about probably did not even take place. If the worrisome situation did develop, you probably handled the problem and moved on.

How much energy do you expend trying to avoid "rain" in your life? Although we all know that rain is an important part of what life brings, we still use our time and energy worrying about what might happen. But when the "rainy" days do come into our lives, we are capable of handling the cloudy weather. We have the skill, we have the support systems, and we have the faith to get through the tough times. And worrying about what might happen did not develop any of the skills needed to face the challenge.

Remember the famous saying, "Worry is like a rocking chair...it can keep you very busy, but it doesn't get you anywhere." Resolve to trust yourself to be able to handle whatever challenges life brings you. Reach out to the community around you if you need help. Then, let go of any tendency to worry about what may happen. You may live to be older than 113!

Begin a new approach toward things that may bother you. Find a jar and place it in a prominent place in your office or home with a stack of small sheets of paper. Each time something comes up that causes you to worry about the outcome, stop what you are doing and write it down. Put those worries into the jar and promise that you will deal with them later, dismissing them from worry for now. At the end of the week, analyze how much energy was saved by placing your worries in the jar. Notice how many of those things are no longer an issue. You may want to consider keeping the jar and renaming it "My God Jar," committing to turn over potential worries to a higher power.

"I don't worry about the storms, I am learning to sail my own ship."

—Louisa May Alcott

"Referral marketing has been the absolute key to our success as financial advisors over the past 20 years. Being able to confidently and consistently articulate our value proposition to our clients and their immediate circle of friends, family, and centers of influence has allowed us to reach and serve the people who need and appreciate what we do the most."

—Gary Wulf
Morgan Stanley Smith Barney
The Woodlands, Tx

Ancient mariners used a sextant to navigate the ocean. This device required the captain to find the horizon and a heavenly body to gauge their location and direction. We can also use personal horizons to navigate our life.

When striving for the desired destination, countless things happening around you may strive to distract you from reaching your goals, but if you "sail your own ship," it really doesn't matter.

Jim Gillespie, a trainer and coach, teaches that you can have "reasons" or you can have "results." If you are unable to accomplish your dreams, you can be certain that you will have many very legitimate reasons why you were not able to get there. You tried, but the storms came, the car broke, the dog ate your homework—something happened that pulled you away from your desired destination.

It's important to know you will get off track on your way to your important goals. Few people go directly from where they were years ago to great heights of success without experiencing a few detours along the way.

Think about an airplane traveling from Houston to Hawaii. On its way to the islands, it experiences turbulence that requires a change of altitude. Then it encounters strong winds that cause the plane to adjust the speed. Several times on the way, the plane is "off course." But the plane's auto pilot system allowed it to adapt to the unexpected over and over again until it lands in the Hawaiian paradise, the intended destination.

Have you let storms throw you off course? Gary Keller teaches that if the "why" is compelling enough, the "how" becomes easy. Review your weekly goals. For each major goal, make an extensive list of why you want to achieve that goal. Include a list of who will benefit from the achievement. Also, record the consequence of not reaching the desired destination. Summarize your results in your journal.

"I'd rather be a could-be if I cannot be an are; because a could-be is a maybe who is reaching for a star."

—Milton Berle

What profound wisdom contained in Berle's jumbled words! So many people play it safe in this world. Many have been hit very hard by a change in retirement funds. They are facing the need to return to the marketplace. Although this unexpected loss of savings is tragic, it can be an opportunity to do things differently. Delayed retirement can shift the focus to a more significant purpose.

Someone once said that his worst fear was to die with his dreams still within him. When you drive past a cemetery, think about how many of the gravestones are for people who were going to take a few risks—as soon as Susie graduated from college, or retirement was available, or a certain bill was paid, or some other legitimate reason to delay living with gusto.

Spreading the word about this incredible way of making your business significant is one way to live a life worth living. Reach for it. Claim it for your own. Decide to work only for those who will appreciate your superior level of service and ask your clients and friends to refer everyone they know, confident that you are not only adding to your bank account but also delivering the best possible exchange for valuable goods or services.

How do you want to be remembered when you pass on to the next life? What legacy will you leave? Take time to write your own eulogy as you would like to be remembered. When you are finished, examine how much your daily activity is demonstrating those goals. Determine to make needed changes today. Reach for a star! Enter in your journal your "eulogy" and your estimate of how your current activities are helping you reach your life goals.

"Everybody is a center of peace or a center of turmoil."

—Reverend Christopher Ian Chenoweth, founder of PositiveChristianity.com

As you step into the world of the referral mindset, you become more than just a salesperson. You become more than simply a business owner who wants to obtain more business. You have become a Leader. You lead your fellow business associates who want to build a significant referral business with you. You lead your clients in understanding this new (old) approach to creating a sphere of business influence.

With this awareness comes the source of your influence on others. Gone away is the urge to pressure a client to make a decision today (because you need a sale today in order to pay the mortgage). Instead, you have trust in God and trust in other people to send business your way. Your confidence in others is palpable to them. You become "a center of peace," and they respond with wanting to be around you and contribute to your success.

This sounds very simplistic and, to some, even unrealistic. But take a few moments and think of times that you enjoyed the process of buying from someone, or a person with whom you gladly do repeat business. More than likely, the person who comes to mind is calm and unworried about where his next dollar will be made. It is not the calm that comes because of the money—it is the money that comes because of the calm.

Take a sheet of paper and draw a line from the top to the bottom of the page, dividing it equally into two parts. Place the word "Peace" in the right column and the word "Turmoil" in the left column. Each time you encounter another person during your day, simply place a hash mark in one of the two columns. Whether the encounter is with your spouse or with the clerk at the fast-food counter, make a decision whether you were in a place of peace or turmoil. (Do not stress over it, because you will surely have some encounters where you were the source of turmoil.) At the end of the week, take time to fully engage in the results of this study. What can you do to increase peace in your business world?

"Courage is the first of human qualities because it is the quality which guarantees all others"

—Winston Churchill

This way of doing business requires you to "put yourself out there"—to become vulnerable. You are asking your clients for more than today's business—you are asking for a relationship. It is a level of commitment that goes beyond client satisfaction. It goes way beyond meeting all the required or even expected actions.

It takes a great deal of courage and confidence to step from behind your advertising and marketing techniques to reveal the person you are. It takes even more courage to develop systems that deliver consistent, dependable service to your clients. Still, it takes even more courage to ask each client to believe in you enough to tell family and friends to use your services.

A referral based business is one in which you feel good about the service you are providing. It is achieved when you have developed value equal to or greater than what your clients expect, and you charge them accordingly. You reap the benefits of working with very satisfied clients and receiving their appreciation in the form of a referral to others. No "high profit" business prospers long term without developing a long list of quality referral clients. In today's impersonal, fast-paced society, it takes courage to see the long-term value of developing referral relationships.

Make a list of businesspeople with whom you would like to develop a long-term reciprocal relationship. Share your vision of a successful referral based business. Ask for their insights, suggestions, and the kind of referrals they are seeking. Immediately find referrals to send their way. Follow up each meeting with a personal note that expresses your gratitude and promises a commitment to this new (or newly confirmed) referral relationship. Record your experiences in your journal.

"Conditions are never just right. People who delay action until all factors are favorable do nothing."

—William Feather

Many people lose enormous opportunities because they had "paralysis from analysis." Every day decisions are made that will not be available at any time in the future. You will benefit from recognizing those special circumstances where you must move forward without doubt or hesitation.

When purchasing a car, you can learn about the manufacturer, decide on colors, options, etc., and what price will fit your budget. Then if you get cold feet and decide to wait until next month, you can probably get the same car and, pretty much, the same price.

But not all good business decisions allow us the luxury of time. Many highly-skilled, successful small business owners will testify to the value of being able to move forward quickly when they see a lucrative opportunity.

The world is in a constant state of change. The factors for making a decision may change in a very short time. If you tend to need all the factors to be "just right," you can miss the opportunity of a lifetime.

Making a paradigm shift in the way you seek business can be immobilizing. You may feel that you want to shift the focus of your business, but you must wait until you have a little more money in the bank, or you've gotten that perfect employee in place to free up your time.

Legitimate reasons for delay will not cease; they will simply change. But you will always have another factor that needs to be "right." Is there ever a better time to make the change than now?

What factors are stopping you from implementing a referral program to the fullest? Relate the significance of these barriers compared to your long-term goals. Stop waiting for conditions to be just right and move boldly forward! Celebrate your success and acknowledge the steps you are making toward change in your journal.

"Change does not come without action."

—Allen Hainge

Most people resist change. They would rather continue to do business as they have done in the past than to address what needs to be done to adapt to a changing market. Then there are those who recognize the needed changes but continue to study the situation without taking action. These people suffer from what is often called "paralysis of analysis."

With everything in a constant state of growth and renewal, the fast pace of change has made us all feel a little uneasy with making decisions. The decision to replace a computer is the perfect analogy. No matter when we decide to replace our current technology or what product we decide to buy, we can be assured that a new product will be faster, cheaper, and better within weeks of making our decision.

However, the folks who go ahead and make a decision continue to get ahead of the pack. As you build your community of referral sources, it would be good for you to recognize those people who are willing to step out there to take action. This type of person can spot a trend toward the referral mindset.

Do you find that making decisions and taking actions are becoming increasingly difficult for you? Use this week to identify the three most critical things in your business that need to be decided. Take them one at a time, list the advantages and disadvantages, and then make a decision. Slot the time to accomplish this delayed task. Budget the money you need. Now do it! Know that your decision is the right one and you can cross that delayed action off your list. Doesn't that feel good?

"Concern yourself not with what you tried and failed at, but with what is still possible for you to do."
—Pope John XXIII

"When people see that you are on a mission and when they can easily tap into that vision with you – they are eager to help you and offer referrals. When people understood that we had a vision to help people overcome failure and rejection they were on board with that, it was tangible. I think that's one reason why the word of mouth and referral marketing we have had on the book has been phenomenal."

—Andrea Waltz
Coauthor, *Go for No!*
Orlando, Florida

Have you ever asked anyone to join you in something you believed in and were met with excuses or even outright rejection? Since you will be involved in a new way of approaching business development, you will find times when it seems that no one else "gets it" and you will be tempted to give up on creating your magical business.

In those times, it is important to think about what is possible. Is it possible to create a community of people who can support and encourage each other? Is it possible to offer your clients such exceptional service that they are eager to recommend you to their family and friends? Is it possible to live in a business world where your clients already believe in you on the first encounter, making every client relationship rewarding?

I believe that all those things are possible. I have seen it work for others and I'm certain that it can work for you. It is all a matter of focus and discipline. You must focus on the global goals and have the discipline to carry out the daily tasks that will get you closer to those goals every day.

Affirm your possibilities this week. In your journal, make a list of "I am" statements. At least ten should be easily written in your journal. Statements such as: "I am prosperous," "I am attracting people to my business every day," "I am worthy of meaningful business relationships," etc. Read those affirmations every morning before work. At the end of the week, record your experiences in your journal.

"Being responsible sometimes means pissing people off."

—General Colin Powell

Developing a significant business based on referrals requires a certain amount of leadership. One of the sure ingredients of leadership is that not everyone will support your decisions.

A friend of mine who is in real estate tells this story: She was interviewed by a rather disrespectful property owner. After he canceled the first appointment within fifteen minutes of their scheduled time, he would not set a certain time to discuss selling his home. Instead, he wanted her to be available immediately after he called. In other words, he expected her to keep afternoons and evenings open until it was convenient for him.

When he called to move the appointment a third time, she gathered enough self-respect to tell him that she didn't believe that she was the best agent for him. He was so mad that he called her manager in an angry rage. He considered it inappropriate to refuse his business.

What she recognized was that other clients, the ones who supported her business with referrals to good, considerate clients, would suffer if she continued to work with this man. In addition to her own self-respect, it was critical that she be willing to let go of a potential commission of several thousand dollars in order to service her good clients with all her heart.

I think she should be proud of herself for that decision.

Are you willing to make some potential clients or customers angry in order to serve your A+ clients? Think about the energy you are currently using in an attempt to satisfy a few unreasonable and demanding customers. Make your "D-list." On it write all the customers who drain your energy and irritate your staff. Now, have the courage to delete them from your service list. Take responsibility for creating an environment of prosperity by weeding out those who do not increase or support the capacity for growing a significant referral business.

Consistency

Consistency Is Like Comfort Food in Business

Consistency is the comfort food of business. Think about it. Comfort food is essentially something familiar that you like, enjoy, want, and expect can make you feel better.

Don't you want your customers to think of your business in that way as well? If they feel comfort with you, they will keep coming back because they see the benefits. When they see benefits, they will share what they have found with others and be your best form of advertising.

In business, everyone also knows that if people don't like your business, they will also tell people to avoid you. If they are going to talk about you anyway, make it a positive experience.

Put another log on the fire or warm up the cocoa. Be the comfort food of business. Add some consistency today. It's a recipe for success.

"To learn is a natural pleasure, not confined to philosophers, but common to all."

—Aristotle

The principles outlined in this book are very simple. It seems that anyone can "get it" and simply apply these principles to his daily business. If the concepts are so good, then results will come without learning anything more. Or so it seems.

Reality is another thing. I have been applying this basic concept to my business, in one way or another, for more than a decade now. Ari Galper, known as the "World's #1 Authority on Trust-Based Selling," reads dozens of books each month. He is totally committed to life-long learning.

He compares his knowledge to having tried many paths in the past as he found his way through the darkness. His role is to take a flashlight and shine a light on the best paths, so that we may learn from his experience. Millions have changed their ways of selling because of what he teaches.

From his home base in Sydney, Australia, he recommends reading, masterminding with others in small groups, listening to CD's, going to seminars, and continuing to learn nonstop.

The pleasure of learning becomes more and more natural as you incorporate it into your daily habits. It brings richness to your relationships that cannot be found without the enlightenment of disciplined learning.

What are your learning goals for this year? Decide which books you will read or what CD's you will listen to, how many trainings or seminars you will attend. Add these to your calendar for the year to create annual, monthly, and weekly goals. Analyze your progress and reward yourself for accomplishing each step along the way.

"The usefulness of a cup is in its emptiness."

—Old Chinese Proverb

Sometimes people become so accustomed to doing business in a certain way that they become their own worst enemy. I'm sure you have heard the saying that all growth comes outside your comfort zone. Whenever we become willing to change what is not working in an effort to find what works, we will find the best solutions.

For years, small businesses have thrived on local media advertising to communicate their message. Now, local radio stations are almost nonexistent, newspaper advertising has become both expensive and ineffective, and direct-mail return rates have plummeted below two percent. If you have not taken the route of embracing technology, I encourage you to follow your clients to the Internet and e-mail.

Early in this journey to a referral based business, you recognized that the ways of marketing your business locally are no longer effective. You have followed the methods outlined in this book to build relationships with individuals who can send you referrals. Now, you can take this same concept of community building and apply it to today's computer-savvy customer. Small companies around the globe are using e-mail to create loyal repeat business. This way to connect with clients is the natural extension of the relationships we have established in our face-to-face connections.

Create a contest for your clients and customers in which they enter their e-mail address for a chance to win. Respond to each entry with a note of thanks via e-mail. You can start small and respond manually, but if your e-mail list is large, you might want to hire a company that provides an auto-responder service to assist with e-mail campaigns. With these e-mail addresses, you will begin to develop your community electronically. Next, you can build a Web site, an e-mail marketing campaign, a blog or a newsletter, or all of them. The purpose of embracing technology is to expand the community established by the practices you have learned previously.

"Many of life's failures are people who did not realize how close they were to success when they gave up."

—Thomas Edison

The magic of the referral process is the cumulative value of your work. The client you take marvelous care for today can bring you dozens more over the years. The business associate you set up a referral partnership with at the next meeting could be a resource for years to come. However, the true measure of the success in this way of doing business takes time.

It may be discouraging when business is not coming at a pace that you feel it should. You may be tempted to abandon the effort in favor of the fast-paced, "colder" version of acquiring business. But that would be similar to abandoning all of your retirement investments in order to buy something you think you need today, like new clothing.

It is possible that you will need to move into this process in stages. Because you are accustomed to food with your meals, it may be necessary to make a few cold calls when you begin. But think of your referral efforts as your long-term investment in your quality of life and keep those activities growing. Just as your investment grows exponentially with compound interest, your efforts to develop a referral community to support your business will yield great profit to you.

In your journal, create a time-budget analysis for the week. Just as you would analyze your money-spending habits in order to extract some funds to place in a long term-investment, spend this week documenting where you spend your time. Anything that uses fifteen to twenty minutes of your time should be recorded. At the end of the week, compare the time you spent on unimportant activities, serving less-than-appreciative clients, and working with "cold" prospects. Carve from that time a budget of referral-building activities. Set specific goals for what you will do to increase this "long-term investment" in your good clients. Record those ideas in your journal and create systems to support the changes.

"We want to live in the present, and the only history that's worth a tinker's damn is the history we make today."

—Henry Ford

You must be committed to the disciplines of developing a community for your referral business to grow. Ask yourself these questions: Have you called people to let them know how important they are to you and your business? Have you written personal notes thanking people for their time helping you? When was the last time you "popped by" to visit people who you know believe in you and your service and have recommended you to others?

If you cannot recall the answers to the questions above, then you are not making the process happen. The normal "cold" way of acquiring business is known for bringing in business by simply calling on a lot of prospective clients—the referral business requires a lot of work as well. But instead of asking for business from people who do not know you, you are asking for referrals from people who know you and like you.

Both ways of business require work. In fact, the referral business actually requires more of you, initially. Because each client is a potential source of more business, you are held to a higher standard of quality.

> Take some time to review your database this week. Next to each person on your list, log which ones you have called, written a note to, or personally visited in the last three months. If there is anyone who has been neglected, make sure that you take action today to remedy the situation. Develop a tickler system that will remind you to drop a line, make a phone call, or visit your clients on a regular basis.

"The quintessential component of superior performance in every activity is the focus of attention."

—Tim Gallwey, tennis coach and author of **The Inner Game of Work**

Chaos...it has almost become an expected part of our everyday life. But it seems that those who are achieving more are able to pick and choose whether to allow the chaos to enter their lives. They are able to tune out the disorganized and disorienting surroundings because they are sure about their goals. Things happening around them fade into insignificance because they are focused on the eventual goal.

It takes a disciplined mind to accomplish the kind of focus that is sure of its ultimate goal. In his book *Start with Why*, Simon Sinek shows us that the *how* becomes easy if the *why* is compelling enough.

In his description of this powerful idea, he tells us that "people like Martin Luther King Jr., Steve Jobs, and the Wright brothers might have little in common, but they all started with why." People can find inspiration capable of changing the world when they harness the power of "WHY."

What are the reasons you would want to develop a business built from a community of people who will refer business to you?

When you become clear about what the above-described lifestyle would bring you, it becomes easier to pick up the phone, call that referral source, and deepen that relationship. Write a paragraph in your journal about how your life will be different when you have achieved your goal of referral business. Write it in the present tense with specific dates. It may read something like this: "Today, (name the date), we sent out the invitations for our client-appreciation party. Now that we have achieved our goal of referral business business, we have so much to celebrate..."

"We must see time as a tool, not as a couch."

—John Fitzgerald Kennedy

Time is a totally indiscriminate tool, yet it is the most vital tool for determining whether you lead a life that is significant or simply pass your time until death. You see, we are all given precisely the same number of hours in each day. Bill Gates, one of the richest men in the world, has the same number of hours to accomplish his goals as does the clerk at McDonalds.

If you are not getting what you want out of life, you must first look at how you spend your time. Our nation is becoming obsessed with "reality shows." Scores of people come home from a job they do not enjoy and watch people compete to see who can be the most selfish, greedy, and backbiting in order to win. If the "reality" of the shows was not disturbing enough, the reality of the individual lives of the viewer is much worse.

The reality is you can choose a life of significance and meaning.

Get into the habit of carrying a small notebook and record how you spend your time. If you have trouble monitoring your time, invest in a small timer or set one of your electronic gadgets (cell phone, computer program, or even an alarm clock) to alert you as each hour passes by. Pay attention to each segment of time. Are you using it as an effective tool? If you keep a log for a week, you may be surprised by what you learned.

"Success is something you have to put forth the effort for constantly. Then maybe it will come when you least expect it."

—Michael Jordan, basketball superstar

"Referral source marketing is one of the three types of marketing I teach and implement in my business and have been doing since I started. That's what I do and it works but you do have to take the time to do this. That's the hard part of course."

—Katrina Sawa
The JumpStart Your Biz Coach
Orangevale, California

Often people considering shifting their focus to a referral-based business ask me, "How soon can I expect to see the results?" If you will begin the disciplines on a regular basis, you will see results immediately. Michael Jordan saw results of his practices immediately, but he did not reach superstardom overnight. It took years of daily effort to become the sports idol he is today.

Where he is today is a reflection of all his daily choices and actions in the past. The same is true in any business. When you choose to spend time on menial, unimportant tasks instead of spending time with your referral sources, you are robbing yourself of the opportunities that would result from the effort.

In a recent prosperity seminar, the speaker outlined the tasks necessary in order for the participants to discover prosperity in their lives. The many tasks were time-consuming and required a great deal of faith. He related several stories of people for whom wonderful things happened seemingly "out of the blue" after they had not only taken the seminar but performed the tasks prescribed in it.

It is no accident when success comes into your life. You cannot predict exactly when it will happen, but if you "put forth the effort" on a daily basis, your life will be blessed with an explosive business.

List the things you are doing to increase your referral business, like writing notes, calling past clients, adding specific services, using certain follow-up activities, having lunches with referral sources, or any number of activities you currently perform. You may even want to include some activities you are not managing to get into your day presently. Now, from that list, select three things that you are willing to do daily or "constantly." Make these activities an "A+" priority of every business day. As you cultivate these daily habits, your business success will come when you least expect it.

"Time sneaks up on you like a windshield on a bug."

—Jon Lithgow

What will you do with the one thousand four hundred and forty minutes you have today? Will you spend it taking care of all the seemingly urgent needs or will you choose to spend time moving yourself toward your important goals?

We have all considered these questions, but few of us are using our time as effectively as we would like. So what causes us to feel like "a bug on a windshield" at the end of the day? We ignore the advice of Stephen Covey in his book, *Seven Habits of Highly Effective People*, and get bombarded with all the "urgent" but not important tasks of the day. Covey encourages us to begin with the end in mind and most of us understand the concept.

The sneaky aspect of time allows us to lose control in the face of this moment's tasks. The end of the day is blessed with satisfaction when your activities represent your highest priorities.

Review your goals in each area of life then write five goals each in the five categories of life: Family, Business, Financial, Personal (physical and mental), and Spiritual. Closely examine your priorities and select one goal from each category. Create a "mini-poster" on 8½" × 11" that lists those five highest priorities. Make seven copies of this poster and place them in places around your home and workplace to keep them highly visible. Let these posters remind you to keep first things first and gain control of your time this week. At the end of the week, record your observations in your journal. Did you see a shift in your priorities?

"The pain of discipline weighs ounces. The pain of regret weighs tons."

—E. James Rohn

Discipline comes very hard for many of us. We want to succeed, but doing the right things on a regular basis becomes too routine. It is so easy to find excuses why you can't do it "today." Then tomorrow comes and sometimes the excuse of yesterday is replaced with a new one. Before too long, the disciplines are abandoned altogether and you find yourself struggling to get by.

The relationships that will grow your business are not casual. Although the leads for business are "warm" rather than "cold," they come from showing your respect for the referrals by treating them with discipline and appreciation. It has been said, "The difference between 'casual and causal' all depends on where 'u' land."

It is easy to become casual with referral sources. If these people begin to feel that you are taking them for granted, they will lose the desire to send you referrals. Instead, your actions should be causal in prompting them to think of you when the chance arises to send you a referral.

Identify the businesspeople who have earned your loyalty. Is their relationship with you casual, or do they put forth the effort to "cause" you to come back to use their services again? In those businesses that cause your loyalty, what disciplines are they demonstrating that you could adapt to your business and consider making them a part of your daily behavior?

---

*"The cynic knows the price
of everything and the
value of nothing."*

—Oscar Wilde

Many people are filled with an awareness of all the things wrong with the world. They will be quick to look at how bad things are and also quick to find someone to blame. Although these people are not likely to be the ones who are excelling in their field, they rarely feel that it has anything to do with their own behavior or attitude. It is always someone else who is being unfair that causes their ineffectiveness.

The price of developing a successful business by referral is a commitment to the daily tasks necessary to make your A+ clients know that you need them to send you referrals. When you first begin, it is common for people to feel that it is a sign of weakness to ask for referrals. Often, it feels rather desperate to talk to people about the advantages you offer and educate them on the reasons why they should refer.

When you find yourself struggling with that issue, it is helpful to think about the alternative businesses that a client might use. You offer something superior in quality because you are planning to make the relationship long term. Some of your competitors see each individual sale or service as having a definite start and stop time, with no long-term relationship. They may even be satisfied with delivering poor customer service if they are paid for their work. Imagine the disservice you are giving your clients by *not* encouraging them to suggest your products or services, rather than leaving them to find someone offering less. Your clients deserve a complete understanding of the value you offer. Educate them and they will be happy to help build the magic in your referral business.

Develop a "Unique Selling Proposition." This USP is commonly talked about in marketing circles. It is a statement about your business that separates it from the competition. It is the essence of what makes you different. Create a statement about the value you offer your clients and make it a point to effectively communicate that value in such a way that your current clients are compelled to tell others.

Positive Outlook

What Attitude Are You Spreading?

Your attitude rubs off on your existing and potential customers, your staff, your suppliers, your investors, and all those in contact with you.

If you maintain a positive attitude, it will be infectious and those around you will pick up on your positive energy. Everyone in your company will feel positive and customers will want to do business with you. In turn, your positive attitude will lead you to maximum performance of your business.

With a negative attitude, the opposite is likely to happen. People will not want to be around you, your staff will feel demotivated, and customers will not want to buy from you. The performance of your business will deteriorate.

With a positive approach, you will feel in control and confident. You will perform at your best. A negative approach will damage confidence, harm performance, paralyze your mental skills, and may also impact your health.

I have met both positive and negative business owners, and it is evident to me that those who approach any economic climate with a positive attitude are seeing their businesses perform better than those with a negative attitude.

"Give it out in slices and it will come back in loaves."

—*"Mother" Buffini*

Brian Buffini, of Providence Systems, teaches referral systems to real estate professionals. The quote on the facing page is one he shares from his mother. I have proved this simple, homespun philosophy in my own business, and it is the underlying theme of this book.

Reciprocity is the foundation of the referral way of life. You will reap many rewards from the referral community if you follow the process. First you must give to others. The next step is to ask of them. As a natural response to the first two actions, be prepared to receive.

Cycles are a basic law of nature in our God-created world. Our lakes and rivers, for example, give up the water in the form of evaporation. The water collects in the atmosphere and then falls back to earth as rain to nourish people and plants while cleansing the surface of the earth.

Remember: give first, then ask, then be ready to receive. The concept may be simple, but your blessings will be abundant.

Imagine this week is the beginning of a paradigm shift in the way you acquire clients and customers. First, create a referral database of clients. If you already have a current list of clients, with name, address, and phone number information, your first step is to select the type of client you would like to duplicate and select those who are most likely to give you a referral. If you have not yet compiled that list, or do not have it organized with complete information, this is your first priority. These potential referral clients will be the new source of your prospects. It is with these people you will give referrals, ask for reciprocity, and experience the joy of receiving.

"I merely took the energy it takes to pout and wrote some blues."

—Duke Ellington

"I believe in keeping a positive outlook in all situations. When I lost everything I had in Hurricane Katrina, I kept a positive outlook by focusing on what can come out of this situation. I stayed focused on my dream of assisting women leaders and those aspiring to be leaders to not be stopped by their circumstances or obstacles; however to live the dream they have inside them; that burning desire to do something or further what they are doing by using their own natural gifts and talents. I shared with everyone I met my dream and did not focus on my tragedy.

"By talking to everyone I met and many people begun to help me and telling others, I was able to build a global business and I am now living my dream of empowering women all around the world.

"The key is to have a positive outlook, believe in your vision and stay focused no matter what the circumstances."

—Valeri Bocage
Founder/CEO of Powerful Women International
San Francisco, California

Redirecting the energy that is causing us stress can give marvelous results. My mother was a strong advocate of the old saying, "idle hands are the devil's workshop." When she had things on her mind, you would always find her sitting at her quilting frame, busy creating a beautiful masterpiece. That was her way of taking the worries of the day and making them valuable to others.

Don't allow your energy to be used for pouting—or anger, frustration, and disappointment. These feelings will drain you of the energy you need to serve your clients. Instead, redirect that energy toward something useful by tapping into your natural gifts.

You have gifts and talents that are your birth blessing. When was the last time that you reflected on the blessings you were born with? If you are fortunate, you can use those gifts in your business every day. If the business is not fully utilizing your gifts, then take the frustrations you face and pour that energy into something that fuels development of your gifts. In return, you will get a marvelous stress reliever and a magnificent use of your talents. The world will be a better place because you invested your energy in alignment with God's intent.

Although you may not have Duke Ellington's musical talent, you are God's child, endowed with gifts and abilities that are valuable to this world. Discover your gifts. If you have trouble identifying them, ask the people who know and love you. Once you become aware of those awesome, God-given gifts, find a way to use them for the purpose of redirecting energy that is currently used in frustration and anger. Every time you feel disappointment, use that energy to create something wonderful in your life! Be aware of how you are using this method of rechanneling negative energy and the changes you are seeing in your life.

69

"Both poverty and riches are the offspring of thought."

—Napoleon Hill

Scientific evidence supports the premise that many people have known for centuries: Your thoughts create your realities. Some will question which comes first. Does the positive attitude create success, or is it the success that creates a positive attitude? I believe it begins with a positive thought. We all have heard of people like Christopher Reeve, who chose to be positive about his health challenges, while others with similar disabilities waste away in anger and self-pity.

"I think; therefore I am." Descartes's phrase has been handed down for centuries and has many implications about how diligent we must be about what we think. It is imperative that we recognize negativity when it comes into our minds and replace it with positive, uplifting affirmations. As a creator of your own riches, you carry an awesome responsibility.

Not only are you altering the fate of your own prosperity, but you are influencing the climate of the world around you. People in your referral community are drawn to your positive outlook on life. In response to your optimism, they will pass the cheerful attitude on to others and the phenomena will multiply. Just like the ripples in a pool of water reflect the expanding influence of a small stone tossed into it, you can become a powerful, positive force in the world by simply controlling your thoughts.

Carry your journal with you and record each time you think or say something negative. For the greatest impact, enroll others to help you recognize those negative thoughts and statements. For one week, agree to pay them a dollar for every time they catch you making a negative statement. Recognize the result of those negative thoughts and immediately replace them with creative, positive affirmations. Focus on eliminating negative, poverty-creating thoughts from your life and check in from time to time to make sure you are staying on track and not falling back into old habits.

*"You can complain because roses have thorns,
or you can rejoice because thorns have roses."*

—Ziggy

Rejoice! We have a beautiful world, an exceptional country, and an opportunity to accomplish virtually anything we desire. It is painful to hear some of the things said when my path crosses the path of negative thinkers—those who know the thorns better than the roses.

Early in my life, I wished that someone would acknowledge me and my love of flowers by bringing them to me. At age forty, I decided to acknowledge the things that brought me pleasure and bring them into my life as often as I can. I demonstrated that resolution by picking up some fresh flowers every month or two. I would use the occasion to celebrate some small success or to cheer me up if I had experienced disappointment.

Now that I am now sixty, I buy them more often. The pleasure of having fresh flowers in my home brightens the way I look at the rest of the world. I can't look at fresh flowers without feeling a smile cross my face. They are a little messy and they require a little maintenance to keep them for as long as I do. But the pleasure of seeing God's wondrous beauty inside my home is worth the cost, the bother, and the looks that I often get when I tell people I am buying them for myself.

It's a good life!

What can you do to bring more pleasure into your life? Have you stopped to smell the roses recently? Examine ways to bring more pleasure into your life. Is it chocolate, fine wine, or flowers? What are those things that bring a smile to your face? Select a few to incorporate into your daily life and quit expecting others to provide them for you. This action will result in a better outlook on life and equip you with a contagious positive attitude that attracts the highest-quality clients.

Ethics and Values

Keep It Real!

One of the most important attributes for small business success is practicing good business ethics. Business ethics, practiced throughout the company, become the heart and soul of the company's culture. Those values can mean the difference between success and failure.

Business integrity and reputation is something that is built up over many years. It can also be destroyed incredibly quickly with one bad decision or half-truth. While publicity is crucial to every business, social media changes the way we work and build relationships. To preserve a good business reputation, extreme caution should be exercised in the area of social media.

Your own personal integrity can guide your organization's integrity. As a business owner, your staff looks to you to set the example. However, the integrity of your organization also relies on those you have working for you. It's not just customer service, either. Everyone from the shop floor to marketing and public relations can jeopardize your business's integrity.

And YOU set the tone for all of this.

"What you are speaks so loud, that I cannot hear your words."

—Emerson

"I have built strong connections throughout areas that I would never have been able to reach without referrals. People that know me know I have high standards and would only be aligned with a company that represents my own personal high level of standards."

—Keri Shaw
Provision Rx
Houston, Tx

When you are building a business by referral, people will notice whether you are doing what you are claiming to do. This reality reminds me of someone living in a small town who tries to make everyone think that he is something other than what is easily observed. The foolish person may think that no one notices the incongruence, but everyone knows. In a small town, though, they may care enough about other members of the community to let it go.

Sometimes we think that we can get by with pretending to be what we believe to be "a better person." In truth, the better person is who you are deep inside. You were put on this earth with a very specific gift structure. You have the choice to be the very best YOU possibly can. Or, as John Buffini would say, you may "become a broken or bent version" of who you are. When you are congruent with yourself, people will see what a wonderful creation God made in YOU.

Does what you profess to be consistent with the image you project to everyone else? Make a list of twenty-five one-word characteristics you possess. Carry the list with you and take it out, frequently, to reflect upon the following question: How are my actions congruent with the words on this page?

77

*"There is nothing noble
in being superior
to some other man.
The true nobility is in being
superior to your previous self."*

—*Old Hindu Proverb*

The referral way of doing business is sure to bring out the true nature of your character. Being a part of something greater than yourself reveals your motives. The scarcity mentality lets people think in terms of beating someone else or being better than the competition. Believe that the world is full of rich prosperity and you will attract that richness to you.

Unfortunately, many people have divided their lives into three stages. When they are young, they go to school and learn. When they become an adult, they go to their job and earn a living. When they get a little older, they retire on the money that they have saved.

The reason why I say "unfortunately" is twofold: First and foremost, this way of thinking places the learning stage very early in life. At the point of adulthood, many stop seeing the need for continued learning. The pinnacle for improvement occurred very early in their lives, and now it is a matter of tolerating the "job" until retirement.

What can you do to improve yourself? Is there something you can learn that would offer greater service to your clients? Is there a skill you could develop that could make you a better person? Think of two to three ways you can improve yourself. From that list, select one that really comes from your heart. Commit to developing that skill, reading that book, or beginning that exercise program.

"Honesty is the first chapter of the book of wisdom"

—Thomas Jefferson

Every day, clients and customers are being told lies. No one intended to tell a lie, but a promise was made to provide a service by a certain time or of a certain quality and the client is given something less. The promise became an unintentional lie.

A business becomes significant by giving full value to its clients and customers. The quickest way to alienate a client is to overpromise and under deliver. Although outside forces seem to pressure you into doing your work perfectly while being faster and smarter, there is a level at which that is not really realistic.

Notice the number of businesses that are providing exceptional services while demanding the highest prices. Many companies charge significantly more than their competitors for the simple fact that they are honest in the promises given. It is obvious that the American people are willing to pay for getting their expectations met.

Look at your own business. Are there gaps between what you and your employees promise and what you deliver every day?
In your journal, make a list of the gaps you observe. What can you do to bring consistency and integrity to those promises? Put systems into your business to assure that your clients are receiving the highest level of service *every time*.

"Character is like a tree and reputation is like its shadow. The shadow is what we think of it. The tree is the real thing."

—Abraham Lincoln

When we think of those we most admire, those with impeccable character come first to mind. What we may not realize is that these people, whom we know to be of the highest character, have not always been recognized in this way. There have undoubtedly been times others have had opinions and/or created rumors that cast a shadow on the reputation of these admirable individuals.

We must learn to let go of the opinions of others. The negative reputation that people hope to create about you is more about themselves than it is about your true character. We each see life through a filter that incorporates our past and skews our perception of the current situation. The people who cast doubt on your character can rob you of your energy and attention. It is much better to let the opinions of others shrink away, as more light is shed on the issue.

Your character, the real thing as Lincoln stated it, has roots in the essence of your intent. It grows out of your love and sincere concern about others. It bears fruit in the good that nurtures others. It magically duplicates itself in the community as you continue to share your good character with those around you.

Catch yourself as you think of people based on their reputation. Notice whether you know if the reputation is based on truth or gossip. Don't "buy into" what has been said about them. Talk to them so you can determine, for yourself, whether your life would be improved by knowing them better.

"We are pencils in the hands of a loving God, who is writing love letters to the world."
—Mother Teresa

"Don't look at what you can get, but look at what you can give. It will be much more rewarding in the end."

—Glenna Griffin
World Ventures
Conroe, Texas

We have all been blessed with the statement "God is love." It is much harder for us to recognize that God is within each one of us and that we are responsible for demonstrating love on a daily basis. It's an awesome responsibility. As the old song goes, "What the world needs now is love, sweet love. It's the only thing that there's just too little of."

A successful referral business requires touching lives at a deeper level. Our goal should be nothing short of literally being instruments of God's love. With that mindset, we will attract more business. Not only will the business be larger in quantity, but it will also be richer in quality.

We occasionally need to think about what we want people to say at our memorial service after we passed on. Is it important for them to say that we were able to get a lot of people to use our goods or services? Do you want people to review the balance in your bank account at your funeral? How much more significant a legacy would it be if people spoke of how deeply you impacted the lives of others while you were building a business?

It is through recognizing our important role of being demonstrations of God's love that we earn the legacy of love. I think it is a very worthy goal.

Pay attention to the way you demonstrate love toward others. Try to make each encounter with other people a positive, uplifting experience for them. Take the time to notice two things. First, record those people who demonstrate love toward you and express your appreciation for them. Second, be aware of times when you are an example of God's love.

"More will get 'caught' than gets taught."

—Joe Neigo

We can tell children how things should be until the end of time, but what they see us doing speaks much louder and leaves a much more lasting impression.

The same is true when we are building a referral networking system. As we carefully select people to belong to our referral team, they will be watching closely to see if we are actually doing what we are professing to do.

Integrity is a vital part of developing a significant business based on mutual trust and reciprocal referrals. You must be very clear about your own values. That requires you to spend some time analyzing what is important to you and then comparing your actions to your priorities, checking for congruence. Having those two aspects of your life in alignment will allow you to live your life with integrity.

The trust that you earn from your referral sources will bring prosperity in so many ways—in money, in a feeling of significance, and in the rich relationships that you make with others along the way.

Who have you "caught" wisdom from? Give people a call this week to tell them how much you appreciate the example they have shown toward you. Tell them specific examples of where they have influenced you in a positive way. Following up each call with a personal note will also let them know that you are willing to go above and beyond to acknowledge a significant referral source.

"This, above all, to thine own self be true – then it must follow; as the night, the day, thou cannot then be false to any man."

—*William Shakespeare*

Authors with the gift of Shakespeare are said to act as God's mouthpiece. His statement about integrity has been around for centuries yet still touches the souls of millions of people.

What does it mean to be true to one's self? To me, it is recognizing that God has a purpose for each and every one of us. We should not compare ourselves to any other person. We can only be the best we can as individuals.

Many young people in their early 20s drop out of society to "find themselves." At the time, it is often more of a rebellion against society than an effort to find the essential self—the glorious demonstration of God's creation. Many of those same people start truly finding themselves as they wrestle with more important questions about the significance of their lives and their relationships to others.

With maturity it becomes less important to rebel against anything. It is much more important to find that our lives actually stand for something. We want to know that the world is a better place because we were born into it.

This kind of significance does not have to cost a bundle of money or require a whole lot of time. That legacy can be created—one day at a time—by following the principles of doing business by referral.

Take fifteen minutes to think about some unique qualities you possess. Examples may be: trustworthy, honest, dependable, hardworking, etc. If you need to, ask friends what words they would use. Extend the list into the characteristics that you find unique and valuable to others in your business.

"There are three main drivers of client loyalty: the value you add; the degree of trust you develop and going the extra mile."

—Andrew Sobel, author of **Making Rain: The Secrets of Building Lifelong Client Loyalty**

"Bottom Line is: All of my current Coaching Clients have come through referrals. By Visioning who my perfect client is (similar values and level of integrity), remaining positive that those who are ready to receive my services are present, and consistently creating relationships through my community involvement, I am constantly grateful for all the meaningful work that is mine."

—Phyllis Miller
Image For Success Business Coach
Bellaire, Texas

What kind of added value do you offer your current clients? Your core value to them is what you explicitly contract to do for them. When you add something to your service over and above what is expected, your clients will respond with pleasant surprise. That surprise value is what they will be telling their friends about you.

It is important for your clients to have a "story" about you. If a former client mentions your name to a prospective new client, he cannot say that you did an "OK" job. Simply performing as he expected is not sufficient for him to go around being a cheerleader for your services.

Each client or prospect will have something personal that is valuable to him or her. Some will value you spending time with them talking about their business challenges, while others will see more value in your ability to remember the names of their children. You want to be attentive to hearing where a client perceives value in service from you and then deliver exceptional value that he will tell everyone about.

We have heard it said, "There is not a lot of traffic on the extra mile." You know, from personal experience, that people who are willing to give extraordinary client service stand out because of their rarity. If you can deliver service that is a cut above their expectations, you can enjoy the reward of long-term client loyalty.

Define the extra mile in your business services. What can be done to add value to your services on a regular basis? Create a list of value-added services and of times that you have an opportunity to go the extra mile. Select a few of those activities to incorporate into your business immediately. Record your list of "Extra Mile Services" and refer to them frequently as you continue to grow your business.

---

*"I slept – and dreamed that
life was joy.
I woke – and saw that life
was but service.
I served – and understood
that service was joy."*

—Rabindranath Tagore

Let's face it, organizations continually struggle with recruiting volunteers. If people knew the joy that comes from making a difference in the lives of others, they would be flocking to good causes, eager for the benefits of becoming significant.

The "Pareto Principle," aka 80-20 Rule, is true in business just as well. In other words, when there is work to be done in any organization, eighty percent of the work is done by twenty percent of the people. It would redeem the eighty percent who do not help, if they were just sitting out for this one function. But it is usually the same twenty percent who are involved in each of the tasks that need doing.

Those involved will tell you that they get great joy from being a part of the organizational activity. They will give testimony to the pleasure of serving. Since I have always been one who volunteered, I can only guess why people choose to sit out when there is satisfying work to be done.

I have heard all the "reasons." They usually have to do with being busy. Do they think that people doing the work are less busy? In fact, statistics show that if you want a job done, you have the most success giving it to a busy person. I sometimes wonder if the eighty percent who don't get involved see the twenty percent who do as working for no gain. If they do, it is a shame. Their limiting approach to service robs them of the pure joy of being involved and making a difference.

Take a look this week at the volunteer service you are performing. If you are not currently involved in some nonprofit service, spend time investigating organizations in your area. Pick a group to begin serving and see what joy it brings, not to mention the possibilities of a referral for your business.

Vision

Dream with Passion

Vision and strategy are both important. But there is a priority to them. Vision always comes first. Always. If you have a clear vision, you will eventually attract the right strategy. If you don't have a clear vision, no strategy will save you.

Through the years, I had learned that if you think about strategy (the "how") too early, it will actually inhibit your vision (the "what") and block you from thinking as big as you need to think.

What you need is a vision that is so big that it is compelling, not only to you but also to others. If it's not your passion, you won't have the motivation to stay the course and you won't be able to recruit others to help you.

"The bigger my challenges, the longer I need to meditate"

—Ghandi

Nurturing your spiritual life is one of the cornerstones for developing a significant business. As I attend business seminars, trainings, and read books on the subject of success, it becomes clear that the people whose lives I would like to emulate have a spiritual practice.

Most life skills training includes recommendations about the five key areas of life: family, business, financial, personal (physical and mental), spiritual. In order to have a successful life experience, it is vital that these five areas be in balance. If one area is lacking focus, all the other areas can suffer.

Spiritual growth can take many different forms. If you don't currently have a spiritual practice, the first exercise is to find your own spiritual center. Start by finding a minimum of fifteen minutes per day to be alone with your thoughts. In that time, allow your mind to clear itself of all the "busyness" of the day. As you take the time to rest your mind, thoughts about the day will rush into the silence. Allow those thoughts to enter your mind and pass through. I personally like to visualize those thoughts being surrounded by a bubble, then floating away. With time, the silence will feel more comfortable to you. You will find that this short break changes your mood and enhances your day.

"This art of resting the mind and the power of dismissing from it all care and worry is probably one of the secrets of energy in our great men."

—Captain J. A. Hadfield

If you are like most entrepreneur business owners, you work about half a day—about twelve hours, six days per week. With this kind of heavy schedule, your business obligations can spill over into your personal and spiritual life. If you let this happen, you will lose in many ways.

First, you will lose your downtime, your time of renewal and "recreation." Without an intentional space for spiritual centering and awareness, you lose the part of you that is essential to your emotional energy.

Second, you lose your connection with family and friends. Sure, your body may be there with them. But if you are still caring more about what needs to be done in your business than you do about those who are important to your life, you lose more than you will gain by financial success. Remember, wherever you are—BE THERE!

The third reason encompasses the other two and adds another ingredient. If you do not rest your mind and spirit—if you do not dismiss work when you are with the important people in your life—you lose energy and are more likely to fail in your business. What a shame!

Pay close attention to your focus this week. Wear a rubber band on your wrist to remind you of your priorities, which are twofold.

First, you will stop at least once a day to rest your mind. Use that break in the day to take a walk, close the door, and close your eyes for a few minutes of meditation or listen to your favorite music. Even if only five to ten minutes, find time to disengage yourself from the demands of your work.

Second, when you are with the important (nonbusiness) people in your life, pay close attention to them. If you find your mind drifting off to the business, take hold of the rubber band and give it a good snap. With each wandering thought, make the snap a little stronger and you will find ways to fully engage with those around you.

"We have treated vision as pretty mystical. It is not. It happens out of how we listen to the world and other people."

—Thomas N. McGaffey, PhD, and author of **The Courage to Lead**

Listening...it has almost become an extinct art. It seems that people feel they must go to a professional counselor in order for someone to truly listen to their needs and desires. In a world with a drought of listening skills, you have an incredible opportunity to quench the desire to be heard.

Clients are often dissatisfied with the level of service from a business. Had they been given the courtesy of listening, the issues often would have been resolved. Tap into the one ingredient that increases the level of pleasure people get from doing business with you and your company—take the time to listen.

Listening is more than hearing what a person is saying in words. Listening is done "with the heart" as well. When you have the vision to truly understand where the need exists, you can become more valuable to your clients than any of your competitors.

With your commitment to developing a referral-based business, it is critical to reach the "heart level" of listening to your clients' needs. They must be able to observe that you truly care about them and their success. They will want to refer you to their family and friends. Because they want the people they care about to get the same warm sense of being valued.

When you are communicating with others this week, be conscious of how much you are listening. Here's a clue: If you catch yourself thinking about what you are going to say when they finish talking, you are NOT listening! Think back on the conversations you had with your clients. Were there times when you were not fully engaged in listening to them? Did you occasionally find yourself correcting your attention and truly "tuning in" to the client? Make note of how your listening patterns change as you become more aware of your thoughts.

"Whatever you vividly imagine, ardently desire, sincerely believe, and enthusiastically act upon, must inevitably come to pass."

—Paul J. Meyer

Many people exposed to this concept of developing a significant referral business will think it is unrealistic. They would like for it to be true, but will be forever convinced that it sounds too easy and that it will never work, not in their business.

I truly feel that any business can benefit from implementing the concepts of the referral mindset. But there is nothing I can tell you that will make it true for you. However, if you just take a moment to imagine being a part of a community that likes you and believes in your integrity and wants your success, then you have an imaginary glimpse of what it could be. Now ask, is it something that you truly desire to have in your business and life?

If you want to have this kind of environment in your business life, you must pursue it enthusiastically. You have to put your heart into the daily disciplines and allow people to see how much you believe in the process and that you are depending on them to support your efforts.

The three-step process is simple—Give, Ask, Receive. Give referrals to other businesspeople and ask them for the opportunity to serve their clients, family, and friends. Then know that the prosperity from your efforts must inevitably come to pass.

Two outgoing referrals will be your challenge this week. In the spirit of "give, ask, receive," you will believe in the natural Law of Reciprocity. Decide on the people to whom you would feel comfortable sending a referral and look for opportunities to refer business to them. Explain your new commitment to doing business by referral and follow up with them to see how the referral worked. Those businesspeople will recognize your passion and belief in the referral process. You have given, you have asked, and now, get ready to receive!

"Tell me, what is it you plan to do with your one wild and precious life?"

—Mary Oliver

How precious is your life? How would your children answer that question? Would your spouse answer in another way? How about your best clients, do you contribute to their lives significantly enough that they would consider your life as precious?

If you had trouble coming up with answers to either of these questions, you may not be planning your life or your business right. You won't often find me saying that a thing is right or wrong, but I am convinced that a life worth living and a business worth having have many moments of being wild and crazy. Regularly doing something that causes you to laugh uncontrollably can keep you healthy. Bernie Seigel made this fact known in his bestselling book, *Peace, Love and Healing.*

When it comes to having a precious life—that's easy! The precious moments are all around us; we simply need to take the time to appreciate them. "Stop and smell the roses" is an often-used phrase, yet many municipal rose gardens have very few visitors. Precious gems are those that bring the highest price at the jewelry store. They are considered precious because of their rarity and because we place value on having them in our lives. What do you consider precious in your life and your business? Do you take time to appreciate your life?

This week, identify some "wild and precious" experiences. Consider calling a client and taking them to a movie during the middle of the day. At the end of the week, you will have some wonderful memories and a deeper relationship with those clients who can make your business grow.

"Are you waiting for your cat to bark?"

—Ralph Wilson, Web Marketing Today

"Everyone is talking about how social media is vital to business building these days, whether you operate on- or offline. I can testify that relationships that I have forged on LinkedIn have helped me advance toward my business goals. One of these relationships led directly to a speaking engagement, the addition of names to my e-mail list, and the opportunity to talk one-on-one with four potential clients. I have been asked to speak before a pre-qualified audience in May as a result of this connection."

—Monique Wells
Toxicology/Pathology Services Inc.
Paris, France

Today's referral based business includes both the personal touch that comes from face-to-face interaction and the electronic community you can create with technology. It is like putting your referral-building methods on steroids when you intentionally establish electronic communication systems that validate and support the goals of your clients.

Once you have come to know your clients on an intimate level, it is time to use your secret weapon to enlarge the net in networking. Take what you know about your clients' needs and apply that knowledge to technological applications. You will want to send regular coupons and/or announcements to your client list. Although your business may be small and local, studies have shown that potential customers may still be going to the Web to find your contact information. Many are more likely to "Google" for your phone number or address than to look them up in the yellow pages.

Not too many years ago, only the Web-savvy and highly-technical companies had Web sites. Today, for the cost of a few small newspaper ads, you can have a Web presence for your business. Many companies are setting up blogs and forums to allow their clients and customers to talk to each other. Facebook and social media bring us together with like-minded people. All these technological wonders are bringing people together on an incredibly intimate level. We used to think that computers would isolate us from each other. What we are learning is that technology brings us together with like-minded people. What better way to build a referral-based community than to facilitate people with the same values, finding common ground within the virtual community of our magical business?

Establish a business plan for your technological communications. Start slowly and give yourself the grace to take one step at a time. Outline the steps you will take to incorporate more community building through the use of social media and other technology marketing. Incorporate this plan just like you would a traditional marketing plan with advertising. Compare results frequently until you identify which works best for you and your industry.

"He enjoys true leisure who has time to improve his soul's estate."

—Henry David Thoreau

Admittedly, when I first began finding a way to increase my referral business, I was only looking for a way to increase my financial estate. I sought to increase my net income by spending my time and money in pursuit of a loyal client base. Years later, I saw that the goal of financial success paled in comparison to the good that it does my soul when clients recommend me to their sons, their friends, and their employees. The confidence demonstrated in the recommendation is magical and worth its weight in gold.

Many business transactions are conducted in a vacuum. Goods or services are delivered in an impersonal way, and although all needs may be met in the exchange, something is really missing.

That is why I equate the referral way of doing business to the days of our grandfathers. There was a time when people were incredibly connected. Each person was highly aware of how his behavior affected the community as a whole. The days of having "barn raisings" seems to be a concept foreign to today's world.

Our grandfathers were very aware of how the soul is nourished by the relationships developed in our daily lives. True prosperity comes from recognizing what deposits we are making in our personal growth account.

You are now going to make a different kind of list, focusing on making deposits into your personal growth account. Set aside time to spend with people who are significant to your personal growth. This person may be a family member, your minister, a respected colleague, or someone involved in a nonprofit organization who could use your help. Try to spend one hour weekly toward activity that will make deposits to your account and experience the joy of the returns.

"Today is the perfect time to dream."

—Author unknown

If you are in a job where you are paid by the hour, your employer may not encourage you to spend time dreaming. You may need to find time "off the clock" to develop and nourish the dreaming part of your existence. I say "find time" although it is not something that most of us find as an essential or even important part of our time management. Some would label dream time as wasting time. I strongly disagree.

Of course, when I talk about dream time, I'm not speaking of what you do involuntarily when you are asleep at night. These nighttime dreams can be valuable as a start to creating dream visions, but I am talking about your dreams of creation. Ask yourself these questions: If money were no object, what would I dream of doing with my life? If I did not have any obstacles of circumstance, how would I spend my time?

Once you have answers to those questions, you can begin the journey of living a life of purpose. By holding this huge, ultimate goal in your mind, your life will change for the better. Your mind will show you the "how" if you can be very clear about the "why."

Envision how you will feel when the dream comes true. How will you be dressed? Who will you be with? Where will you live? What will you be doing? And most importantly, why did you make the effort to get here? Make an entry in your journal that describes in detail your life in three years and read it before starting your day in the morning and before ending you day at night. Remember, clarity paired with emotion will manifest your dreams with speed.

"The thing always happens that you really believe in; and the belief in a thing makes it happen."

—Frank Lloyd Wright

"I have found that by doing things for others in the networking arena I have been able to build relationships with people that provides Know, Like and Trust. By doing this it has given me the opportunity to refer all types of business owners to each other. In return I have been referred to many business owners that has grown my business. This has allowed me to build a bigger business with people with the same ethics, vision and values."

—Tony Gambone
Founder of Tough Talk Radio Networker
Katy, Tx

Do you remember believing in fantastic things as a child? Although there may have been adults who tried to stifle their chuckles, you were confident that you would show them. They would be sorry for laughing at you when you showed them the things you could do!

What happened to that childlike faith in your ability? Did you lose it at a young age, or did it take high school or maybe college to "cut you down to size"? Most of us, somewhere along the way, lost that childish belief in ourselves. We became reasonable and rational. We learned to tailor our expectations to what others were accomplishing.

Famous people like Wright never lost the recognition of his greatness. We all possess incredible talents that have been "cut down to size" by others. We have given away our greatness in order to fit in with the crowd. The people who believe in their God-given gifts and abilities are those remembered by others.

What fantastic things do you believe you can accomplish in your business? Do you believe you can deliver such exceptional service that others will flood you with their referrals? Make a list of your fabulous capabilities. Take caution that you do NOT list your accomplishments. They are not who you are. Finish the statement with: "This is what I believe about myself..." Do not be shy, modest, or humble in this list. No one else will see it. Simply state your belief in yourself honestly and boldly. Come back to the list often and add characteristics as they come to mind.

*"There is no security in life,
only opportunity."*

—Mark Twain

I hope you have enjoyed the journey into the world of referral-based, community-building, continuously-validating and rewarding business. If you have consistently apply this system you will see much progress. You have seen an increase in profits. You have a loyal circle of customers who speak well of your product or service. Marketing that used to be a big expense to bring in new customers is now focused on those who support you and refer your business to others.

It is not time to relax, however. Instead, seize the opportunity to drive that relationship even deeper. Find new and interesting ways to expand your circle of clients. Give more to your referral-building community than ever before. Build on what is working and allow the reciprocity to fill your life (and your bank account) even fuller.

I believe these actions you have taken will bring about spectacular business and personal results. As this way of doing business spills over into more and more aspects of commerce, the world will literally become a better place to live. I know that sounds a bit unrealistic to some. Nevertheless, community building as a way of doing business is showing up all over the globe. If each business will take that trend and make it work for them, we can all be included in thriving business communities. We can create a movement that truly makes a difference to owners of small businesses and to the customers they serve.

Now, go back through your journey and review the actions you have taken. Which ones felt good to you? Which ones brought a profitable response from your customers/clients? Try to remember how you felt about your business future one year ago. Do you feel more optimistic about your business opportunities now? Select the things that still resonate with your passion and develop a plan for the coming year.

About the Author

When you meet Linda Ballesteros, you'll sense that something is different about her and will feel drawn to know her better. You'll immediately know that her energy is positive, engaging, and approachable. As you get to know her, you'll also discover that she is gifted in empowering others to pursue their own dreams. It is this outward focus of being a caring, involved, and valuable friend that most fully describes the Linda Ballesteros so many people have come to know and love.

As a powerful networker in 2009, she attracted more than 300 members to a start-up women's business networking organization called Wine Women and Wealth. Then, as if that wasn't enough, she expanded what was offered to those members by merging with a national organization and served as Regional Director in a growing number of Texas Chapters. Now with her new radio show, *Power Talk with Linda Ballesteros*, she is able to bring her gift of empowerment to many more.

Although many people tap into Linda's natural coaching style, she is really an *UnCoach*, because she brings much more to the process of helping others than the traditional business coaches. She seeks to help people open the *Gateway* to their ultimate selves and explore what is possible together.

Some of the many workshops she has created and taught are Follow Your Bliss, Become a Cash Magnet, and The Women's Empowerment Series, various business related topics, to name a few.

It is easy to see why she succeeded in the banking industry for more than thirty years and why Mario chose her for his wife. They have three grown children and are affectionately known as Linny and Pop Pop to their grandchildren.

Contact Information:

Linda Ballesteros
Linda@LindaBallesteros.com
www.LindaBallesteros.com

Testimonial:

Linda quite simply gets it, when it comes to networking.

Linda and I are both networkers in the Houston metro area and we have known each other for the last three years.

In almost all cases, the organizations we belonged to did not get it. They got maybe twenty percent of it but not the remaining eighty percent.

And you might have guessed that the remaining eighty percent is where the real success is. You must find some people who you "know, like, and trust" to create a joint-venture partnership with. Once you are doing some co-marketing, you can begin to tap into the remaining eighty percent. Almost all networking groups will talk about getting to know one another so you can maybe use their services (first level). The smarter networkers know that it is the people they know that you should tap into (second level). The genius marketers know that the Joint-Venture Partnership is the way to go. Linda knows the ins and outs, and nuts and bolts of networking, and congratulations in finding this book.

—Rus Bel
The Best Geeks
Tomball, Texas

Made in the USA
Lexington, KY
13 December 2017